PLAY
WITH YOUR
FOOD

PLAY
WITH YOUR
FOOD

A Joost Elffers Book

STEWART, TABORI & CHANG

Published in 1997 and distributed in the U.S. by
Stewart, Tabori & Chang,
a division of U.S. Media Holdings, Inc.
115 West 18th Street, New York, NY 10011

Distributed in Canada by
General Publishing Company Ltd.
30 Lesmill Road
Don Mills, Ontario, M3B 2T6, Canada

Distributed in Australia by
Peribo Pty Ltd.
58 Beaumont Road
Mount Kuring-gai, NSW 2080, Australia

Distributed in all other territories by
Grantham Book Services Ltd.
Isaac Newton Way, Alma Park Industrial Estate
Grantham, Lincolnshire, NG31 9SD, England

Library of Congress Cataloging-in-Publication Data

Elffers, Joost
    Play with your food / by Joost Elffers
        p. cm.
    "A Joost Elffers book."
    ISBN 1-55670-630-8 (hc)
    1. Fruit carving. 2. Vegetable carving.
    3. Garnishes (Cookery). 4. Cookery (cold dishes). I. Title.
TX652.E367   1997
641.8'1—dc21   97-16557

Printed in Germany

10 9 8 7 6 5 4 3 2 1

Incredible—they look just like animals!

P L A Y WITH YOUR F O O D

Introduction

"Don't play with your food!" is an admonishment we have heard for many generations. It means, now it's time to eat, don't dawdle, don't procrastinate, don't be disrespectful. But food—especially fruit and vegetables—is often playful in its own right. We have all had the experience of finding an odd-looking vegetable and seeing something other than the vegetable itself: a funny face, a cute animal, a contorted body, a mini-monster, an overgrown insect. Fruit and vegetables seem to invent their own visual puns. *Looking* and *seeing* can be two entirely different things.

For some reason, it seems inherent in human nature to seek correspondences between ourselves and the creatures or objects that surround us. Things constantly remind us of other things. Thus, a fruit or vegetable can look like a mouse or a bear or a human face. This phenomenon seems to echo the modern scientific finding that we all come from the same source and hence have many things in common with other objects around us—even physical resemblances. How many times have we seen a dog owner who looks just like his or her dog? Or a machine that looks like a bird?

Leonardo da Vinci claimed to see all of life in the passing of clouds overhead. There are contours of famous mountains and rocks recognized for centuries as human figures and animals. In a sense, everything we look at is a kind of Rorschach pattern: we see what our unconscious mind wants to see. Einstein believed that while we all view the same things, we all think something different—*he* certainly did! We are always finding surprising, sometimes magical, ways of "seeing" things. And that's what this book is about.

Play with Your Food celebrates our roots, often literally. It trains us to see common and uncommon fruits and vegetables as other living forms, reflecting our own personal (subjective) view of the cosmos. It teaches us not to accept the appearance of things at face value, but to creatively see other possibilities, using the unlimited resource of our imagination.

The goal is to produce new images *suggested* by the fruits and vegetables themselves, with an absolute minimum of alteration: a slit here for the mouth, two slices there for the raised ears, two holes for the eyes. If the original piece has a stem sticking out, use it as a tongue or a nose; if there is a root cluster, like that of an onion or leek, use it as hair or as a beard. The idea is to make a whole new animal, or face, or object—as much as possible—out of the existing "features" of the original piece. That is vegetable nirvana!

Anyone can practice and learn this new way of seeing—from the very young to the very old, from all countries of the world, on any educational level. In this sense, the creative process presented in this book is a most democratic pastime. Even a child is empowered to create *instantly,* to transform one thing into another. To make art out of food.

Bite the Hand that Feeds You

For those who would view the treatment of fruit and vegetables in this book as somehow disrespectful of the poor and the hungry, they are surely missing the point. *Play with Your Food* does not deface and waste the precious food we eat. It is always eaten soon after its transformation. And its new form is designed to heighten the food's appeal—to make it more appetizing and give it more zest than it originally had. Indeed, the creative treatment of a fruit or vegetable is done out of a greater respect for the food's potential than we had previously known. To invent new creatures through our imagination is to raise the food to a higher level—a kind of blessing or grace—prior to the actual eating. This attitude is not far afield of the Buddhist's awareness of and respect for food taken into the body; or the tribal custom (now adopted by New Age adherents) of thanking the food itself before consuming it.

On a more practical note, children who are chronically poor eaters can see food in a new light. They can be amused and entertained by food, making the eating more attractive, more meaningful, and even more fun. They can thank the food—then bite the head off! No disrespect here. Just a different level of awareness.

Here is a camel that may have been reincarnated as a pepper! Do its "roots" go back to the days of pyramids and pharaohs? Or is this just a fluke of nature? We know that we're seeing a vegetable, but once the camel is "identified" it is no longer simply a vegetable. We cannot look at it without seeing the animal—indeed, the two perceptions are now inseparable. Of course, the pepper isn't a realistic camel; it is a comical portrait that our precious imagination creates from the pepper's shape.

Photo Frederic Neema, © Reuters/Corbis-Bettmann

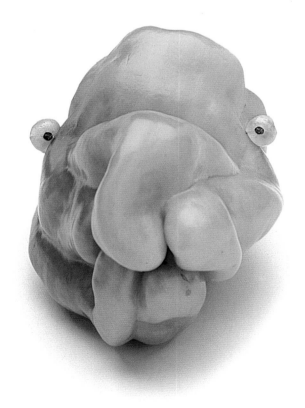

One way we have already trained our eyes to see one thing and interpret another is the common—and entertaining—practice of identifying pet owners with their pets. It seems uncanny, the number of times we've seen a tall, slender, graceful woman, with long, flowing hair, out strolling her Afghan. Or a grumpy-looking, jowly man and his bulldog. Are these correspondences accidental? Is it conceivable that the dog owners were drawn to their pets (or vice versa!) because they already looked like each other? Observers like us tend to think so, whether or not it's logical or provable. Our ability to associate pet owner with pet is identical to the process of seeing living creatures in the shapes of vegetables and fruits. One only needs to look consciously for similarities. It is a fascinating—for some, addictive—game that broadens our smiles as well as our imaginations.

Coincidence or destiny?

There are some amazing correspondences between pets and their owners.

© UPI/Corbis-Bettmann

One source of comic relief in our mechanized and electronic world is the accidental connection between inanimate objects and real-life forms. Remarkably, nineteenth-century English novelist Charles Dickens habitually lent human traits to the machinery of the industrial revolution and, conversely, described many of his characters as automatons. In our environment we are surrounded with man-made objects that often have striking resemblances to living creatures. Oil-well rigs look like giant prehistoric birds pecking the ground in slow motion. Front grilles of many cars and trucks take on the characteristics of human faces. (Remember the old postwar Buicks with their menacing teeth? And doesn't the VW "Bug" say it all?)

Again, all we have to do is look around and consciously seek the correspondences between man-made things and living creatures. Look again at the common staple remover: it is a sci-fi monster about to attack and snap your fingers off! Or the andirons in your fireplace: are they not long-necked minotaurs guarding the entrance to their cave? Here we see a common plug adapter—no! It's a dread-filled face, hair standing on end, beseeching us not to shove the plug in.

The ginseng root has captured the imagination of many cultures for thousands of years, undoubtedly owing to its uncanny resemblance to the human body. Growing from the earth, it seems to symbolize the life force itself.

In the Orient especially, the powers of ginseng are highly prized. It is thought to be a cure for countless ailments and is considered a sexual stimulant.

In Japan, ginseng is thought to cure some cancers. In China, it is considered an anti-aging herb that can also heal ulcers and calm nerves.

Is ginseng's human shape trying to tell us something? Is this powerful herb a plant-form of ourselves—a curative little brother making another wondrous correspondence between vegetables and humans?

Cloud Images.
Top row: three faces;
Bottom row: two hearts
and a face (r.).
Photos © Susan Eder

Clouds are an endless source of imagery for discerning objects and creatures in our world. All of us have, at one time or another, pointed to the sky and said, Isn't that just like a face or an animal or a train? Leonardo da Vinci went beyond that. He felt that if he watched clouds long enough, he could see all of life passing by in their infinite shapes. The more you look, the more your eye will be sharpened to see life elements.

What makes clouds so intriguing is that their shapes are constantly changing. You can see one image when you first focus on a cloud, but it may transform into an entirely different thing as you follow it across the sky.

While clouds may literally change their shape in the sky, it is also possible to create "change" in our mind's eye—just from the way we choose to look at the natural objects around us. Can leaves change into dancing bodies? Trees into grumpy ogres? Lakes into mirrors?

Natural formations in rocks or mountain contours sometimes resemble people or animals. This has long been appreciated by humans. Whether primitive tribes regarded such an occurrence as religious or modern man sees it as a stunning natural phenomenon—it always elicits a sense of wonder in our minds and emotions.

Largely because of the scale of rock or mountain formations, we are awed by their majesty and stateliness. We can't help wonder if Nature (or God) is sending us a possible message—maybe just the idea that something much larger than ourselves is watching over us. We know that we're only seeing a rock (or group of rocks), but it seems so much more than that. Perhaps it's the idea that a thing can be itself but also something other than itself—gaining a new, perhaps higher, significance. Particularly when it is on such a grand scale.

Cap Creus, 1958. *The Slumbering Rock.* Photo Robert Descharnes, © Descharnes & Descharnes

From the Seeds of the Past to the Fruitful Present

The "roots" of vegetable art go back to the sixteenth-century. There was the innovative artist Giuseppe Arcimboldo, who assembled assorted vegetables to create extraordinary facial portraits. A seventeenth-century artist, Charles Le Brun, invented *visionomy,* the science of facial expressions and facial types. Among other things, Le Brun made comparative studies of human faces with animal faces, attributing animal characteristics to humans based on their common features. Some men look like lions, some like horses. Le Brun believed that people took on the traits of their closest-looking animal type. Louis Philippe, the obese nineteenth-century French *roi bourgeois,* was so plump that his head was regularly depicted by caricaturists in the shape of a pear. (The French word for pear—*poire*—also means "fathead.")

Going from real life to caricature or cartoon involves a leap of the imagination. The examples above suggest that there is a special visual connection between person and animal or person and vegetable (fruit).

Is this so different from seeing animals and objects in fruit and vegetables? A real-life pear becomes a pear bear. But the pear bear is a teddy bear, which is already a caricature of a real bear.

Reality can be a blurry thing. The process is often ironic, playful, off-the-wall.

Turning the "Leaves" of this Book

The examples shown in *Play with Your Food* may be copied by the reader (though never literally, since every piece of fruit or vegetable is unique—there are no two peppers alike). The copying is rather a means of getting the hang of this special way of seeing—the process of creating new subjects out of naturally grown foods. Don't be a slave to the examples you see. Use them instead to inspire your own creations.

For those readers looking for specific "how-to" instruction, we have provided a final section of the book filled with hints, tips, guides, and advice. You will learn, for instance, to see a radish as never before. You will cut off the green stems, but leave enough to function as a mouse's nose. Cut a few slices from below so that the mouse can stand without rolling over; and use those slices as two mouse ears.

You'll be advised to look for vegetable shapes that turn most readily into animals. You'll be told that all roots—large or small, clean or covered with a hairy skin—make the best animals. And you'll be allowed to go beyond cute: Some creations can be big scary rats covered with mud!

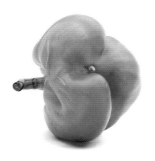

Harvest Your Creativity
In the end, this book presents a very playful way of finding a subject within another object. Isn't this the very essence of the creative process—being stimulated by one set of conditions to resolve (re-solve) them into a new set of conditions?

There is a kind of magic involved in looking at one thing and seeing another. It is not a magic based on deception. Quite the contrary, it is the miracle of seeing a new truth—one that was there in the first place and needed only your imagination to give it substance. A vegetable *garden parade* is exactly what you see—no mystical apparition based on faith. It's a simple visual revelation that says: *a pear is a bear is a pear is a bear....*

This much is for sure: once the reader is empowered to "see" in the way this book presents itself, he or she will never look at a piece of fruit, or a vegetable, the same way again.

So let's dig in—and celebrate our roots!

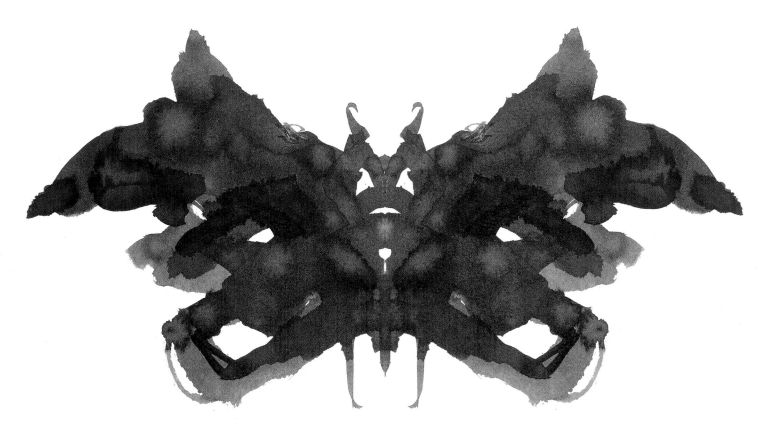

A Rorschach look-alike

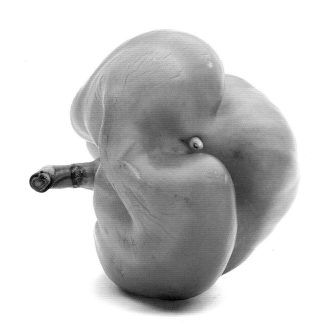

The Rorschach inkblot, used traditionally for psychological testing, is the perfect proving ground to demonstrate that we can see a real thing in an abstract image. Unlike clouds, the inkblot never changes; like clouds, the possibilities are seemingly endless. In its intended use, the inkblot is designed to draw out the unconscious associations of the persons being tested, presumably to determine their true inner emotions—fear, guilt, anger, etc. The possible responses to the inkblot are as varied and complex as the mind itself.

In this book, the Rorschach-like image is meant to give the reader an opportunity to gaze at a random shape and "interpret" it as being any number of possible real-life objects or situations. Is it a moth? An explosion? A set of symmetrical profiles? Is it a microscopic creature—or the Big Bang in the universe? Here's what else the inkblot tells us: we see what our mind wants us to see. This can be one mesmerizing image or a whole set of possibilities. The range is as limited or unlimited as our imagination.

Giuseppe Arcimboldo

The Vegetable Gardener, c. 1590

Museo Civico Ala Ponzone, Cremona, Italy

© Scala /ART RESOURCE, NY

Giuseppe Arcimboldo

The Vegetable Gardener, c. 1590

Museo Civico Ala Ponzone, Cremona, Italy

© Scala / ART RESOURCE, NY

Giuseppe Arcimboldo (1527-93) was a painter of human portraits assembled from vegetables, fruits, and flowers. Known as a "fantastic" painter, he produced a body of work in the sixteenth-century characterized by brilliant, at times bizarre, innovation. His universally appealing art has influenced Dada, Surrealism, and other twentieth-century movements and artists—including the likes of Picasso, Duchamp, Magritte, Ernst, Man Ray, and even Jackson Pollock.

Through his vegetarian vision, he explored man's relationship with himself and with nature. He saw a unique connection between his human subjects and other living organisms. His stunning portraits raise questions not only of what is real (what are we made of?) but how far the imagination can go in our ability to see, then interpret the world we live in.

Giuseppe Arcimboldo (1527-93)
Vertemus (Emperor Rudolf II), 1590
Skoklosters Slott, Sweden
© Erich Lessing / ART RESOURCE, NY

Pumpkin (1997), N.Y.

Would Arcimboldo have appreciated turning a radish into a mouse? A pea pod into an insect? Most certainly. Did he expand the imagination of his contemporaries and of artists (and non-artists) to the present day? Absolutely. Indeed, we may be taking Arcimboldo to the next step: while he used many pieces to create a whole portrait, we use just one to create our work of art!

Let's look at two of his paintings and see how his mind transformed ordinary vegetable matter into extraordinary, expressive human likenesses.

Men/Hoot-Owls
Charles Le Brun

Charles Le Brun (1619-1690) was Louis XIV's court painter. He was also a major theorist on the subject of faces, writing and illustrating a treatise in which he drew hundreds of human faces and their visual derivations from animal faces. In his comparative studies, Le Brun found visual links between specific animals and types of humans—the noble, the evil, the aggressive, the kindly, the intelligent, the submissive, the insecure, and so on. The seventeenth-century artist/scholar went even further by suggesting that humans actually took on the personality traits of the animals they most closely resemble.

For our purposes, the significance of Le Brun's work is in his seeing animal characteristics in human faces. We talk of someone's equine nose, leonine features, hawk-like face or nose, doe eyes, owl eyes, etc. In short, when we look at someone's face we can often identify an animal which he/she more or less resembles. It seems to be second nature to make such connections.

We are also fascinated when we see animals that resemble humans—not just monkeys and apes (our closest evolutionary relatives) but dogs, fish, cats, seals, ducks, and so forth. We are forever seeking and finding visual correspondences with the creatures around us.

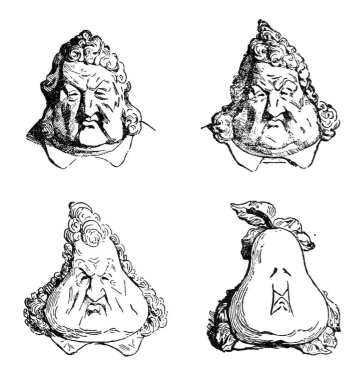

Les Poires
Caricature de Louis-Philippe, 1832

Louis Philippe (1773-1850), the nineteenth-century *roi bourgeois*, was afflicted not only with obesity but with having a head the shape of a pear! A caricaturist of the time created a now-famous sequential cartoon of Louis, showing a kind of slow-motion, four-part transition from king to pear. When a heavy fine was imposed on the editor of the newspaper that published the drawings, the editor wanted to know for which drawing, exactly, he was being punished!

Something to think about—where does the king end and the pear begin? Looking at all four drawings together, even with the changes from one phase to the next, "Les Poires" never loses its remarkable double resemblance to the king and pear at the same time.

Similarly, once we identify an animal or face in the fruits and vegetables we choose for our vegetable zoo, we can never see just one image again. It becomes indelibly both forever. The pear bear, the pepper camel, the radish mouse. That is the beauty and magic of seeing with an expanded imagination.

Is what you see what you see? Or what you make of it, literally? Here is a pear. The pear clearly resembles the head of a bear. Not the head of a real bear, but a teddy bear—which is a caricature of a bear. In our minds, the teddy bear is real, and because of this we not only want to, but we do, perceive the pear bear to be as real as the original pear. The imagination has no bounds!

Teddy Bear, coll. Saskia Voorbach
Photo © Mirja de Vries

Before the conveniences of modern commerce, the pineapple was a rare and exotic fruit, particularly in Europe. For this reason it became the ultimate symbol of hospitality—either to serve to guests or give to hosts of a party.

Here we celebrate the pineapple by carving out a palm tree, its tropical cousin. Once the cutaway portion is removed (and hopefully saved for a fruit salad), you are left with the palm's shape. Notice how the potted tree takes on an entirely different scale from the original pineapple. Transformations can do that. This creation differs from others in the book in that most of the pineapple is cut away from deep inside—major surgery—while the other creatures on these pages are only "skin deep" in their conversion from the original.

VEGETABLE
ZOO
A Garden Parade

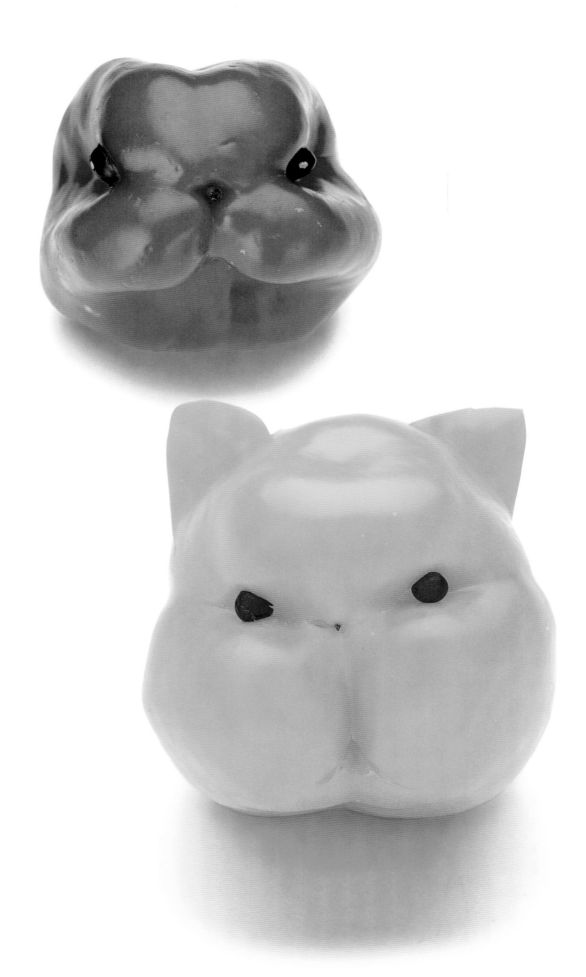

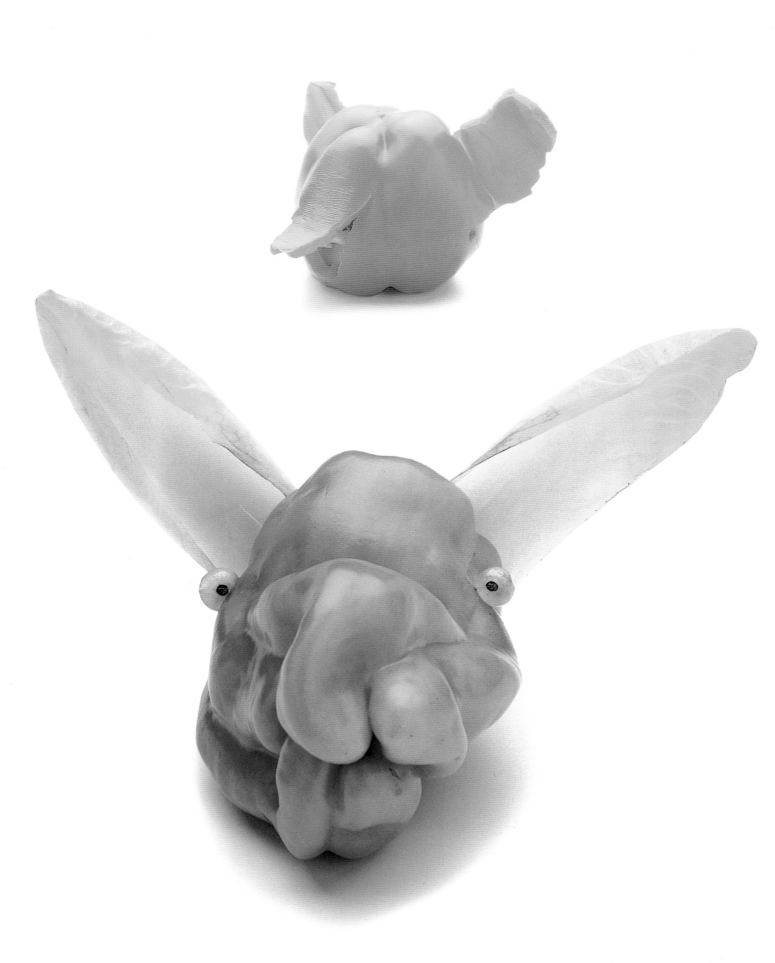

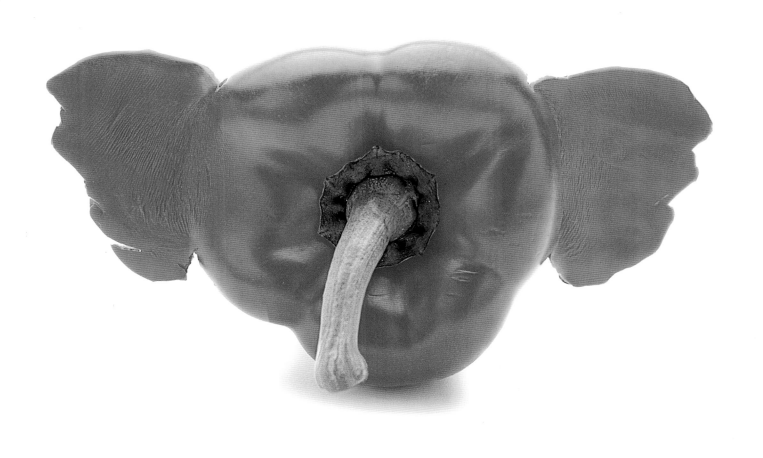

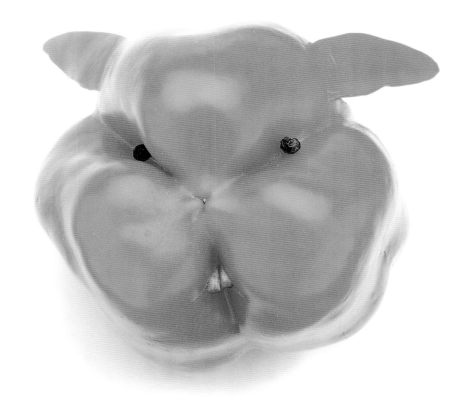

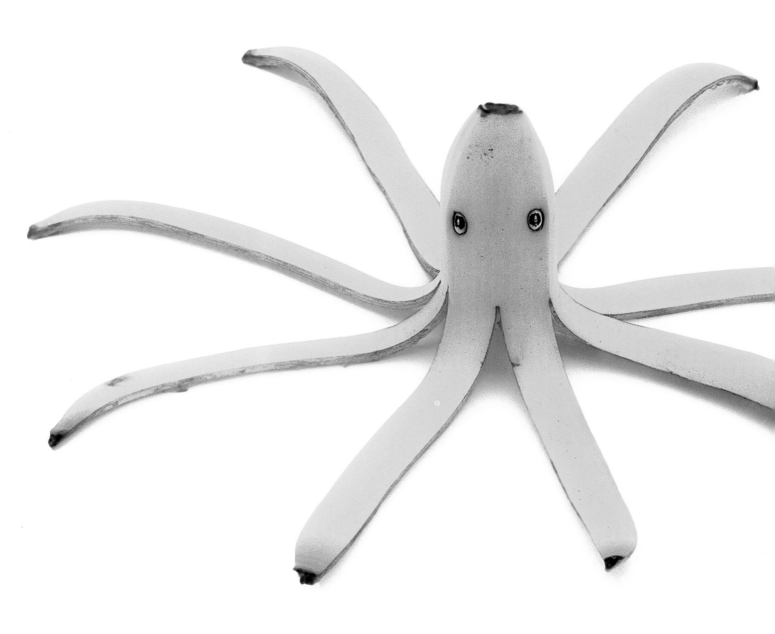

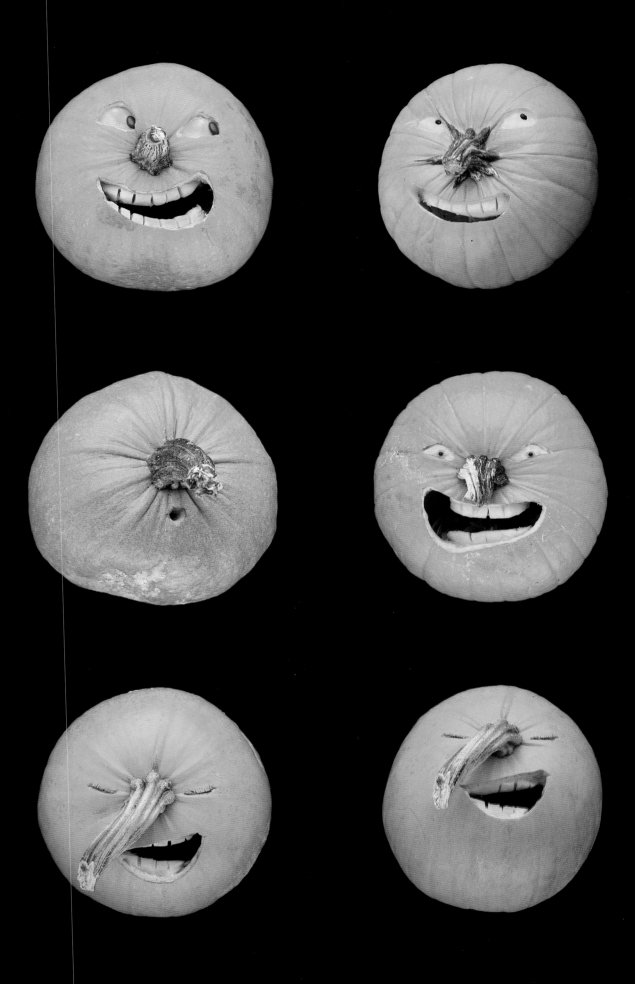

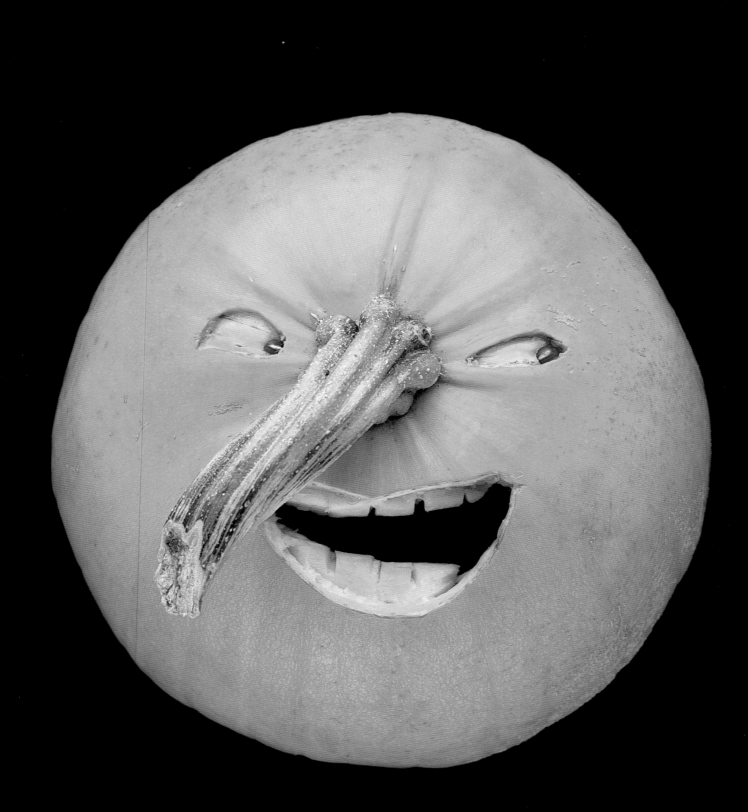

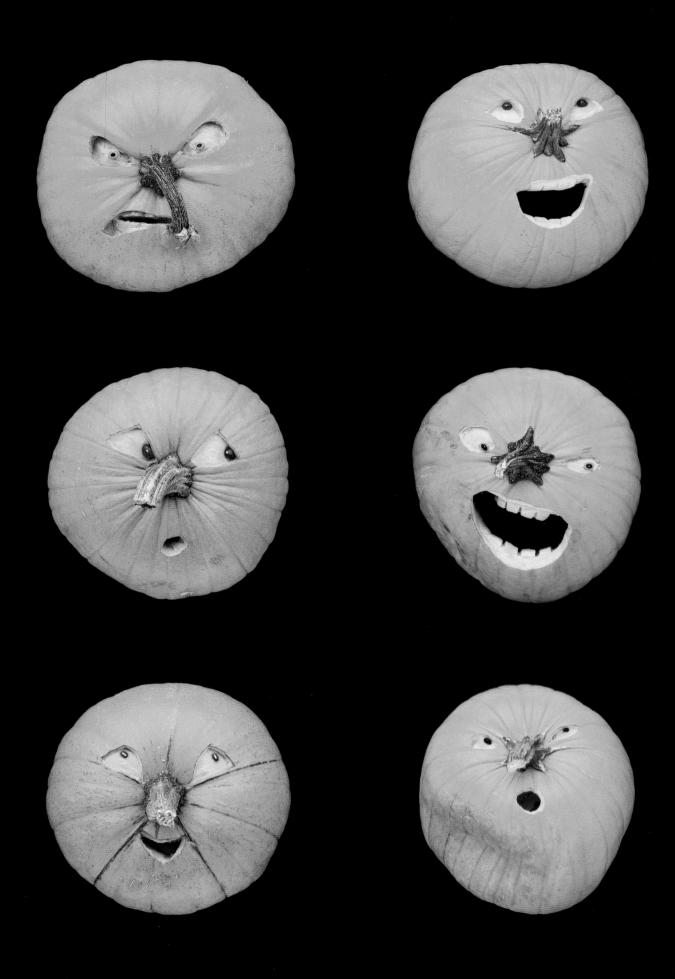

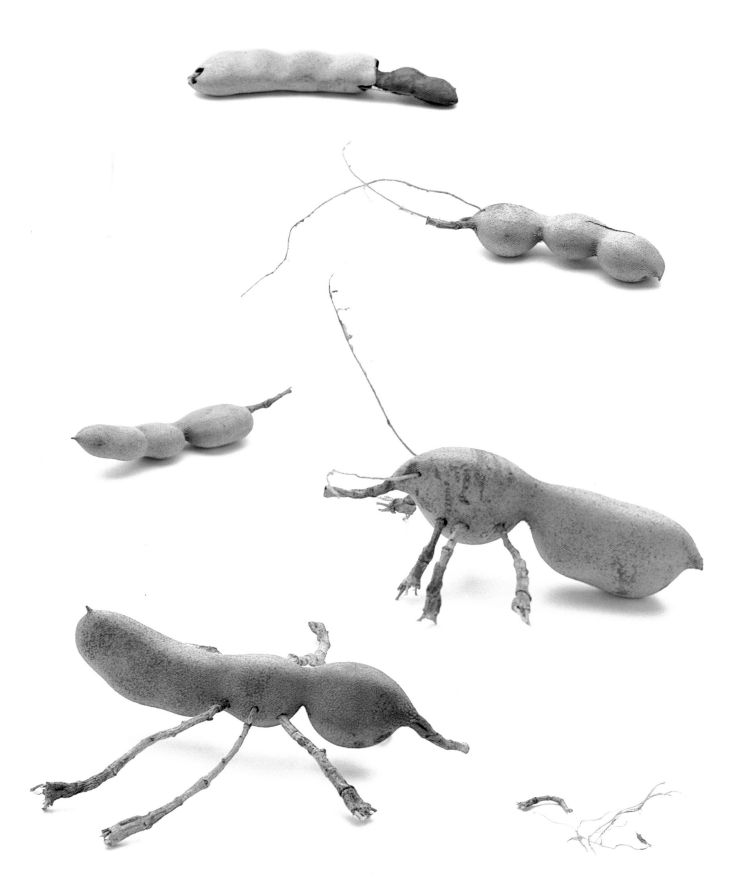

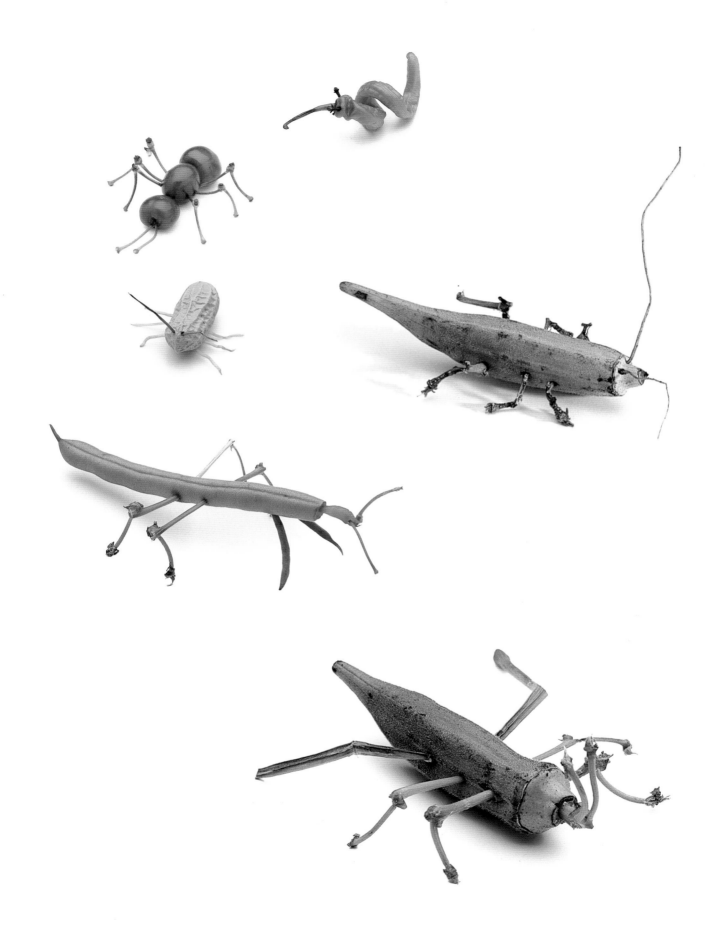

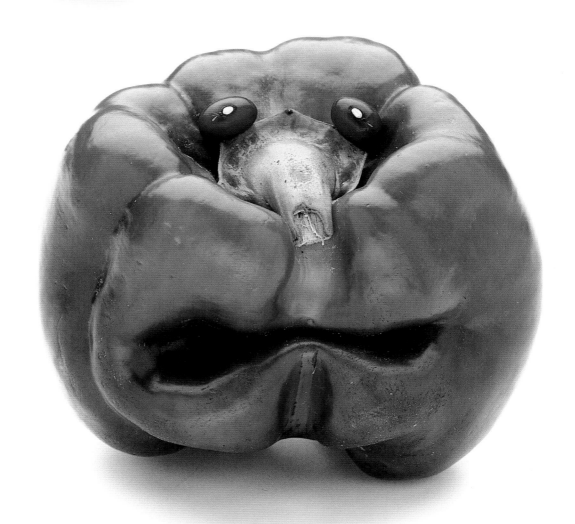

MENU
INGREDIENTS
AND RECIPES

Menu

The following pages contain a catalog of the main picture section in the book. For most full-size creatures, we have here a miniature—and a description of what its "body parts" are made of. This practical guide will enable the reader to see the wide range of elements used to create the simple impressions of eyes, ears, legs, hair, and so forth.

Ingredients and Recipes

It is important to stress that there are no strict rules for creating your vegetable zoo. These pages just offer some helpful hints and tips.

Pineapple turtle
Pineapple leaves are used
to create legs and head

Pineapple bird
Head and tail of crown leaves,
beak of shaped leaves

Gaggle of garlic geese
Most minimal intervention,
just bending the skin to create
heads and necks

Yellow pepper cat
Eyes of beans, ears folded out
from back of pepper

Red pepper seal
Eyes of beans in natural
depressions

Yellow pepper elephant
Cut and folded body parts

Red pepper elephant head
Folded-out ears, trunk is
natural stem

Green pepper camel
Ears of endive, champagne
grapes for eyes

Red pepper rodent
Folded-out ears, teeth of garlic

Green pepper bunny
Eyeless (eyes implied in folds
of pepper), snow peas for ears,
teeth of almonds

Leek freaks
Peppercorn eyes, beet-juice
lipstick

Pear mouse (two views)
Clove eyes, ears grafted from other parts of pear, belly sliced off to flatten bottom, stem removed and re-positioned as tail

Singing scallions
Eyes of crushed peppercorn, beet-juice lipstick

Pear bear
Grapes for eyes, folded-out ears

Sheep/dog pear
With stem/stick it's a dog, without stem it's a sheep

Lemon pigs
One with cut-out mouth, other with natural snout, both with fine-bead eyes

Gai Choy Pekingese dogs
Black olive eyes tucked under loosened leaf

Banana octopus
Black-eyed pea eyes

Banana bird
Wedge-cut stem for beak

Elephant yams (two poses
from one potato)
Trunk-down elephant is
turned upside down to create
trunk-up elephant. Eyes of
round seeds

Anteater yam
Radish root-tip for tongue

Mouse yam
Natural tail

Baby seal yam
Peppercorn eyes

Mole yam
Peeled and folded-out paws

Pig yam
Natural snout, folded-out ears

Melon tortoise
Pepper head

Melon snapping turtle
Artichoke leaves for head
and legs

Gossiping onions
Black-eyed peas for eyes,
beet-juice lipstick

Melon turtle
Okra head

Chile pepper worms
Clove eyes

Tamarind pod bugs
Legs and antennae from
tamarind stems

Tamarind pod insect
Larval stage

Pumpkin faces
Using stems as noses, all kinds
of facial expressions are
suggested in the converging
lines. Variety of beans in
recessed eyes, teeth carved out

Pea pod mantis
Grape-stem legs

Artichoke leaf aphid
Radish-hair legs

Peanut bugs
Turnip-hair legs

Pea pod caterpillar
Grape-stem legs

Grape ant
Jointed grape-stem legs
(all parts from grapes)

Cherry ants
Jointed cherry-stem legs
(all parts from cherries)

Stringbean mantis
Jointed stringbean-stem legs,
antennae of stringbean stems
(all parts from stringbeans)

Okra grasshopper
Jointed stringbean-stem legs,
antennae of stringbean stems

Snow pea cicada
Jointed cherry-stem and
grape-stem legs

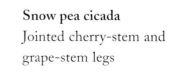

Okra bug
Grape-stem legs, root-tip
antennae

 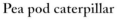

Artichoke coat
Mushroom hat, eyes of beads,
beet-juice lipstick

Mushroom faces
Beans and peppercorns for eyes

Artichoke wolf
Champagne grape eyes,
peeled-up ears

Earless cat
Eyes of beans

Green pepper goblin
Two beans for eyes resting
on pepper

Bok choy bird
Stringbean head

Bok choy lion/buffalo monster
Eyes of beans

Orange cats

Navel orange (eyes closed)

Same navel orange (eyes open),
eyes of beans and
sliced almonds

Navel orange, eyes of beans,
folded-out ears

Strawberry lion cub
Seed or pit for eye

Baby owl melon
Eyes of strawberry slices with
blueberry pupils

Red onion walleyed walrus
Champagne grape eyes

Chayote frog
Beans for eyes

Brussels sprout beetle
Grape-stem legs, snow pea
heads

Brussels sprout beetle at rest
Stringbean-stem head

Brussels sprout pig
Folded-out ears, seeds for eyes

Brussels sprout hippo
Ears folded and trimmed

Red pepper hummingbird
Celery-leaf wings

Brussels sprout whiskered boar
Folded-out ears, sliced
whiskers

Squash goose
No changes

Papaya bird
Okra beak

Squash duck
No changes

Cucumber lizard
Legs carved out
(all one cucumber)

Croaking frog cucumber
Folded-out legs, carved-out
mouth (all one cucumber)

Root crop mice (radishes,
beets, turnips, etc.)
Tails suggest the animals,
greens trimmed back to make
ears, bellies sliced off to make
flat bottoms, beads or seeds
may be added for eyes

Fat cat turnip
Belly cut out to carve legs
from surplus, ears shaped from
surplus and inserted

Mushroom man
Eyes and mouth poked in and
allowed to brown naturally,
mushroom bodies and stems
rearranged

Coconut moose
Ginger antlers inserted into
holes drilled in coconut, eyes
and nose are natural coconut
spots

Brussels sprout goldfish
Folded-leaf fin, leaf tail attached

Choosing Your "Raw" Materials

The best and most represen-
tational fruits and vegetables
for your menagerie can be
found at farmers' markets
and organic food stores.
Organically grown produce
tends to exhibit many
variations in both size and
shape, and thus lends itself
to an easier, more natural
interpretation in "pruning"
it into creative new forms.
In short, organic shapes are
odder, less uniform, and
more exotic than those sold
in commercial supermarkets.
If you have no other choice,
however, the supermarket has

more than enough selection to provide you with interesting fruits and vegetables.

The most important thing to stress in choosing the candidates for your vegetable zoo is the creativity involved in the selection process itself. Standing there amid mounds of peppers or pears or radishes, it is your discerning eye that will determine whether most of the work has already been done by nature—and you will only have to add the finishing touches.

Looking and Seeing

The process starts with your hand-picking that special fruit or vegetable. Rotate the piece as you hunt for the face or animal in the natural form of the food. The goal is for you to select new images *suggested* by the fruits and vegetables themselves, requiring an absolute minimum of alteration. If you make the right choice, you will need only a slit here for the mouth, two slices there for the raised ears, and maybe two holes for the eyes. If the original piece has a stem sticking out, you might be able to use it as a tongue or a nose. If there is a root cluster, like that of an onion or leek, you can visualize it as hair or as a beard. The idea is to make a whole new creature or face out of the existing "features" of the original piece. That is vegetable nirvana!

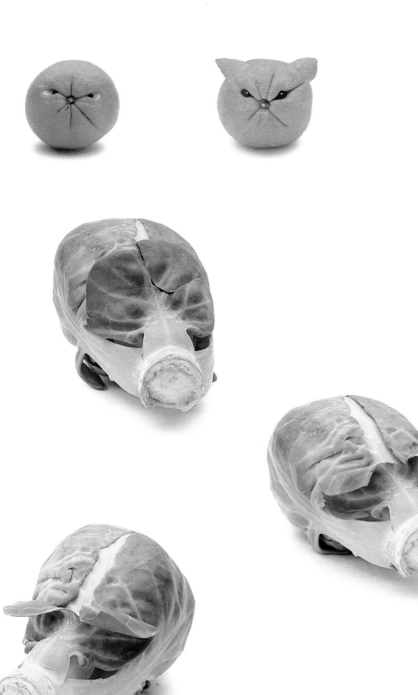

Breaking the Ground Rules

At this point, it is vital to understand that as the keeper of this vegetable zoo, you can take as many liberties as you wish. The addition of beans for eyes, or rice for teeth, or leaves for ears is just a matter of expressing your point of view, or interpretation, of what you first saw in the original piece. These features were *already there* in your mind's eye.

In conclusion, while guidelines are given, this book mandates no hard-and-fast rules. It is okay to combine parts of one fruit or vegetable with parts of another. You even have the freedom to assemble multiple fruits and vegetables to create a whole new image. Be free. Be happy. Play with your food.

*Here is a selection of materials you may find helpful in creating
a variety of body parts and facial features for your creations*

Eyes

Eyes can be the indicators of emotion, personality and mood. A variety of materials may be used, from beans and beads to grapes and olives. Whatever works for you is valid.

In some cases, simple slits with a knife are enough to indicate eyes—no need to introduce separate elements. And in other cases, certain animals or faces may have no eyes at all, but just depressions in the skin of the fruit or vegetable that might suggest eyes.

It is important to look at all possibilities for placing eyes. The starting point is usually the nose, and you work outward from there. Before you actually make holes for the eyes, move your beans or grapes around the face to see the many different opportunities. See how the personality changes as you shift the eyes around—wider apart, closer together, higher, lower and so on.

Some beans even have little dots on them, "pupils" that can add even more personality to an animal or face

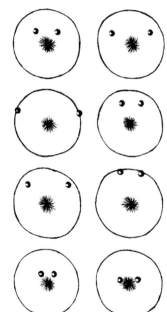

Easiest Method of Attaching Eyes
Once you have chosen the elements (beans, etc.) you plan to use:
– Cut a shallow hole slightly smaller than the eye.
– Push or press the element in. Often the flexible skin of the fruit/vegetable will hold the eye in place.

This is the same yam

Noses

Anything that sticks out of a fruit or vegetable is a potential nose. Noses tend to be *found* (natural) on the fruit/vegetable, rather than made through carving or adding new elements. Once you "identify" the nose, the other features will fall into place. Be sure to rotate the piece and look from every angle to see which is the best position for the nose, i.e., up, down, or sideways.

Plant roots can often be noses or mustaches. A good example of this is the red onion walrus, top row, second from left.

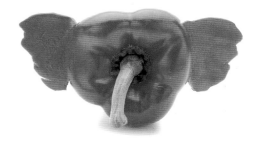

Is this a trunk or a tail?

Ears

Ears can be either cut and folded out or added (inserted) as separate pieces.

To make fold-out ears, outline their shape with your knife, leaving a fairly large area of attachment at the base. Carefully slice beneath the skin and gently roll the ear out from the tip to the base. Patient and gradual rolling will prevent the ear from tearing. For very large ears, don't be afraid to cut far back on the fruit or vegetable. With leafy vegetables (like Brussels sprouts), leaves can be similarly folded out to create ears.

When adding ears as separate pieces, you can cut and shape them from any desired fruit or vegetable—not just the one you were starting from. Once you have fashioned the ears, be sure to move them all around the larger piece to see where they belong best. When you have found the right spots, make the appropriate slots with your knife and insert the ears.

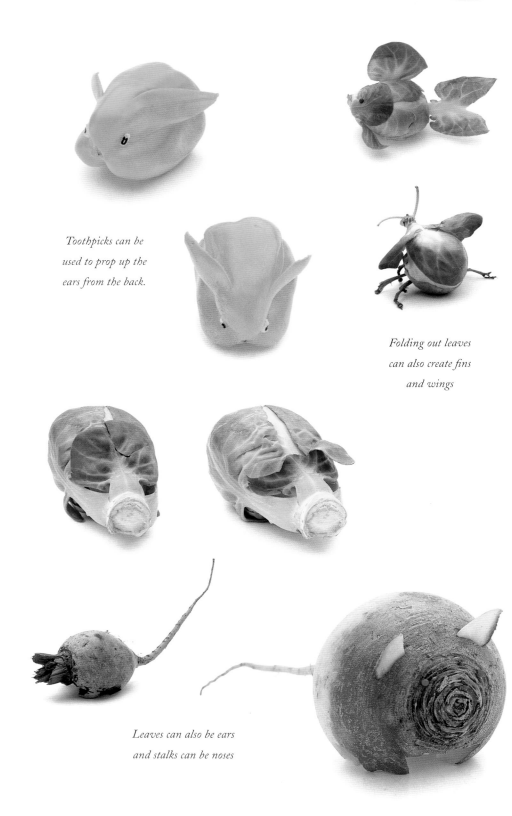

Toothpicks can be used to prop up the ears from the back.

Folding out leaves can also create fins and wings

Leaves can also be ears and stalks can be noses

Mouths

Mouths can be *found* (natural) or they can be made (carved). In some cases they may be minimal, and in others not necessary at all. If you do carve a mouth, start small—you can always make it bigger.

Teeth can be either carved or added (rice, corn kernels, almonds, etc.). When adding, the same technique can be used as for eyes, that is, make holes and press them in.

A slice of ginger makes a great tongue.

Legs

Fruits and vegetables tend to resemble heads more than animals. It is relatively easy to find faces, but more challenging to find creatures, especially animals with legs. For this reason you may have to train yourself to look first for the possibilities of whole animals/creatures.

Legs may be carved by cutting into the fruit or vegetable and slicing away the "flesh" between and around the desired protruding limbs. In other words, the legs are already built into the piece you are carving.

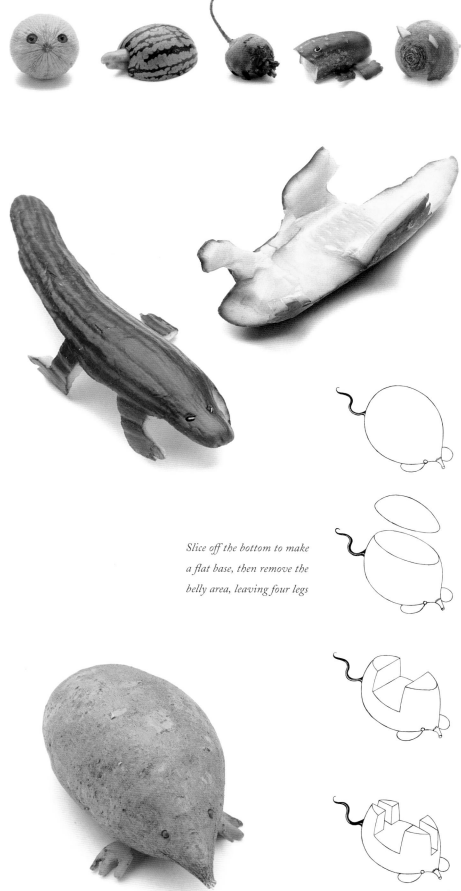

Slice off the bottom to make a flat base, then remove the belly area, leaving four legs

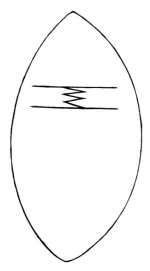

For the purists among us, the paws are shaped with only three cuts

Crawling Insects

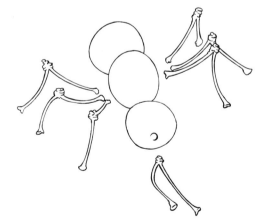

It is quite satisfying to use all parts from the same fruit or vegetable

For the many possible types of insects, legs are critical. Nature has provided a variety of stems that make ideal insect legs, including the leg joints. These stems are found, for example, on string beans, cherries, and grapes. Simple stems can be used for antennae and short straight legs. Jointed stems look great on all kinds of insects. Pick the legs (stems) that look best for the insect you are making. Be aware of the variety of joints, twists, hairs, splinters, peels, etc.

All stems are added to the insect bodies by making small holes and simply inserting. Be careful not to make the holes too large, or the legs will slip out.

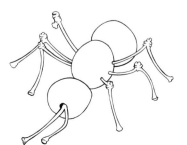

It is important to know that whatever you use for legs, the creatures' bodies need not be raised off the ground. In many cases, stems are not strong enough for such support. It is perfectly all right for a body to rest on the ground, with legs only for balance.

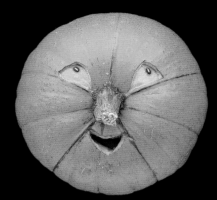

Creases and Wrinkles

In the Halloween tradition carving pumpkins is an established American pastime. However, unlike the traditional jack-o'-lantern, our approach to the pumpkin involves looking at it from a different angle—literally.

Seeing the pumpkin's stem as a nose opens up a whole new world of possibilities. Suddenly all the lines that converge on the stem/nose become lines of emotion.

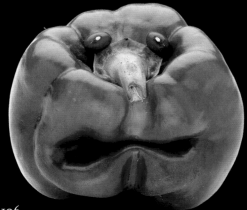

*Whatever is said in this section about
pumpkins also applies to other
creased/wrinkled fruits and vegetables*

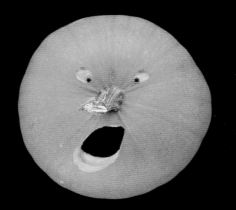 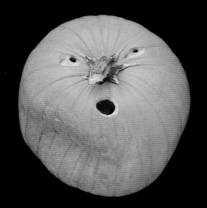 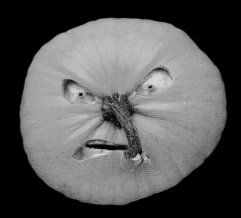

Facial Expressions

The faces suggested by pumpkins may seem angry at first, but not all pumpkins are surly. Their facial expressions range from anger, suspicion, worry, and cunning to surprise, flirtation, jubilation, and bliss.

Even the direction of the nose can reflect different expressions. Try turning the pumpkin around to see the possibilities: nose-up versus nose-down.

  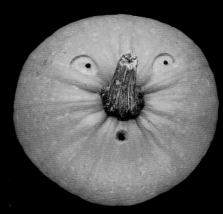

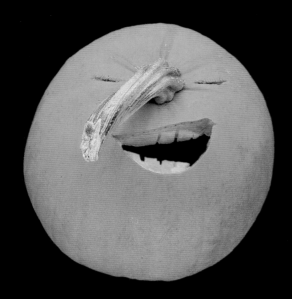  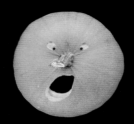 

Cutting and Carving

Pumpkins are very carvable.
When working with them you
will find that shallow carving
of the outer skin will expose
a lighter-colored flesh,
or meat—best for making the
teeth and eyes. Use the lines
and creases to suggest ideas
for facial expressions.

   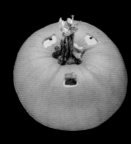 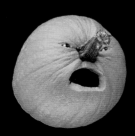

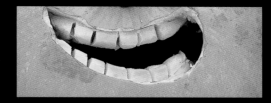

Teeth and Eyes

Try to make the teeth curved, conforming to the round shape of the pumpkin like real dentures—rather than a flat, fence-like facade.

Eye shapes and sizes can reflect many different emotions. Explore the effects of large eyes, slanted eyes, slit eyes, straight-cut eyes, round-cut eyes, and so forth.

When carving teeth and eyes, remember to start small. They can always be enlarged as you are working. In the process, you may stumble upon a variety of expressions and moods. Coincidences are often the best part of inspiration.

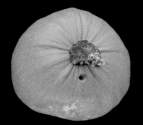

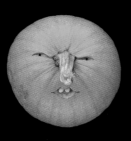

P L A Y WITH YOUR F O O D

Concept and Art Direction: Joost Elffers, New York

Art: Saxton Freymann & Joost Elffers, New York

Text: Mark Gabor, New York

Design: Erik Thé, Amsterdam

Photography: John Fortunato, New York

Lithographer: Litho Köcher GmbH, Cologne

Printer: Druckerei Uhl, Radolfzell am Bodensee

Production Assistant: Eng-San Kho, New York

Special thanks to Wendy Burton

A Joost Elffers/Andreas Landshoff Production